In this glossary:

[a] is pronounced as in far
[e] is pronounced as in get
[ee] is pronounced as in feet
[i] is pronounced as in sit
[o] is pronounced as between got and goat
[oo] is pronounced as in loose
[u] is pronounced as in purr
[y] is pronounced as in yes

[kh] is pronounced as in Scottish loch
[zh] is pronounced as in vision

Other books available from Ethnic Enterprises:

The Raspberry Hut
and Other Ukrainian Folk Tales
Retold in English
by Danny Evanishen

Zhabka
and Other Ukrainian Folk Tales
Retold in English
by Danny Evanishen

How April Went to Visit March
and Other Ukrainian Folk Tales
Retold in English
by Danny Evanishen

Vuiko Yurko The First Generation
by Danny Evanishen

Vuiko Yurko Second-Hand Stories
by Danny Evanishen

I Can't Find the Words to Tell You
by Anne Everatt

Kharkiv
by Zvychaina/Zurowsky/Evanishen

Boris Threeson

and Other Ukrainian Folk Tales
Retold in English

Retold by Danny Evanishen
Translations by John W Evanishen
and Angela Cleary
Illustrations by Deanna Evanishen

Published by
Ethnic Enterprises
Publishing Division
Summerland, BC

Copyright © 1997
Daniel W Evanishen

All rights reserved. The use of any part of this publication reproduced, transmitted in any form by any means, electronic, mechanical, photocopying, recording, or otherwise, or stored in any retrieval system, without the prior written consent of the publisher is an infringement of the copyright law.

Canadian Cataloguing in Publication Data

Main entry under title:
Boris Threeson

ISBN 0-9697448-7-7

1. Tales--Ukraine. I. Evanishen, Danny, 1945-
GR203.18.B67 1997   398.2'0947'71   C96-910453-7

Ethnic Enterprises
Publishing Division
Box 234
Summerland, BC
V0H 1Z0

Printed and Bound in Canada
by New Horizon Printers
Summerland, BC

1 2 3 4 5 6 7 8 9 10•06 05 04 03 02 01 2000 99 98 97

Table of Contents

Boris Threeson 11
The Daughter of the Flower Queen 29
The Death of the Sun-Hero 39
The Devil and the Gypsy 47
The Giants and the Herdboy 55
The Hazlenut Child 63
Ivan Invisible 69
The Lazy Wolf 77
The Lion in the Well 87
The Lute Player 93
The Magic Bird 103
The Man and the Priest 109
The Tremendous Turnip 111
Truth and Lies 117
The Wizard 129

Notes on the Tales 132

Dedicated to the children, for whom the stories are remembered.

Foreword

This is the fourth in the series. There will be more books as long as I can find stories to fill them. That should not be a problem; the Ukrainian culture is very rich, and there are thousands of tales.

I enjoy collecting and publishing these stories, but they are hard to find. Often, people know the stories, but for various reasons don't get around to writing them down.

In this day and age, writing down the stories is becoming more and more important, as the people who know the stories either die or forget the stories. It is up to us, now, to save this very important part of our heritage.

As in the first three volumes, *The Raspberry Hut*, *Zhabka* and *How April Went to Visit March*, some tales found in this book are old favorites, while others are less familiar.

If anyone has any more tales they would like to contribute to future volumes, they could be sent to me at this address:

> Danny Evanishen
> Box 234
> Summerland, BC
> V0H 1Z0.

—Danny Evanishen, Publisher

Acknowledgments

This book, like the first three volumes in the series, is the result of a lot of work by a number of people.

Translations were done from Ukrainian by my father, John W Evanishen, and from German by Angela Cleary. Natalka Evanishen, my mother, provided my very first folk tales and always has lots of encouragement for me. Deanna Evanishen, my niece, did the art work.

Thanks are always due to the libraries and archives across Canada that make their material available. A list of all the stories and their sources will eventually be published.

Thanks are due to Dr Robert B Klymasz for stories in his book *Folk Narrative Among Ukrainian-Canadians in Western Canada*, published in Ottawa in 1973 by The National Museum of Man.

When the stories submitted by various people across the country are published, I will acknowledge their contributions.

Thank you to everyone who sent their stories in to me, thinking I would find them interesting. I definitely find them interesting.

Thank you also to Dorene Fehr, who did a lot of reading and advising on the project, and also took the photograph on the back cover.

— Danny Evanishen, Publisher

10

Boris Threeson

Long ago there lived a man and his wife, who had a son. While working in the fields they left the baby at the edge of the forest, where they could watch him. One day, an eagle came and snatched the boy away before their horrified eyes and carried him away to its nest in the forest.

In this forest lived three brothers and, while one of them was getting water at the well, he heard somebody crying and hurried back to the cottage.

"My brothers, I can hear what I am certain is a baby crying. Let us find it."

The three brothers searched the forest and found the little boy in the nest of the eagle. They climbed up and got the baby. Talking the situation over, they decided: "We will raise this baby ourselves. Since there are three of us, we will call him Boris Threeson."

The brothers cared for the little boy and taught him everything they knew, and he grew up to be big, strong and wise.

One day, Boris Threeson said, "My beloved fathers, the time has come for me to leave you."

This made the brothers sad, and they asked, "What can we give you for working for us all these years?"

"All I really want is a foal," was the reply.

The three brothers gave their adopted son a foal, and he went on his way.

As he walked through the forest, Boris Threeson saw something shiny in the distance. He wanted to see what it was, but he was too tired to walk any further. The foal was still very small, but he asked, "Will you carry me for a short while, little foal?"

"You will have to wait, Boris Threeson. I will tell you when you can ride me," answered the foal.

Finally, they came to the place where the shiny object was. It was a feather from the bird called the Phoenix.

"Do not take the feather," said the foal. "This is no ordinary feather, but the Queen of Feathers. If you do not heed my advice, you will live to regret it."

Boris Threeson did not heed the advice of the foal. He picked up the shining feather and put it carefully into a pocket of his shirt. The two of them walked on and soon came to the magnificent palace of the tsar.

At the palace, Boris Threeson found work in the stables housing the work horses from the fields. While grooming the horses, Boris Threeson brushed them with his feather and their coats became clean and shiny as they had never been before.

The other stablehands were astonished at the change in the horses. They were so impressed with their appearance that they hooked the horses to the best carriage of the tsar. When he saw the magnificent horses, the tsar demanded to know who had groomed them to such perfection.

"Boris Threeson is your new horse groomer, your Majesty. He must have done it."

The tsar went to the stable and sought out Boris Threeson. He asked him, "What magic is this that you use to make the coats of the horses so shiny?"

"Your Majesty, I do no more than the others who work in the stables. I know nothing of magic," said Boris Threeson.

The other stablehands were jealous of the attention the tsar had given the new stableboy, and they wanted to get rid of him. Spying on him, they saw Boris Threeson grooming the horses with the feather of the Phoenix and ran to tell the tsar.

"Your Majesty, Boris Threeson grooms the horses with a feather from the Phoenix. That is the magic he uses. Surely, if he has a feather from the Phoenix, he will be able to capture the Phoenix itself for your Majesty."

The tsar summoned Boris Threeson and asked him: "Is it true that you have a feather of the Phoenix?"

Boris Threeson replied, "Yes, I do."

"Boris Threeson, you must bring me the Phoenix itself. If you do not, I swear by my throne that you will die."

Boris Threeson returned to the stable sobbing, while the other stablehands danced with glee.

The foal came to Boris Threeson and asked him, "Why are you weeping, my friend?"

"How can I not weep? The tsar has just given me an order that the two of us together cannot fulfil."

"You see?" said the foal. "I told you not to pick up the feather of the Phoenix, but you did not listen to me. But listen carefully to me now, and I think I can help you to capture the Phoenix. Ask the tsar for a cup of peas and a bottle of his best brandy. Then let us see what we can do."

The tsar, happy that Boris Threeson was going to get him the Phoenix, gave all that he asked for. Four servants were also sent along by the tsar.

The foal told Boris Threeson to have the servants dig a pit in the field, put the peas at the bottom of the pit, and pour the brandy over them. This was done, and they all hid to watch what would happen.

The Phoenix flew into the pit, ate up the peas and became so drunk that it could hardly move. Boris Threeson caught the Phoenix in a net and took it to the tsar.

"Well done, my loyal servant!" cried the tsar when he saw the shining bird. The tsar was so pleased that he rewarded Boris Threeson with all sorts of rich treasures.

The other stablehands were not the only ones jealous of him now. They said to the tsar, "If Boris Threeson can bring you a feather from the Phoenix, then the Phoenix itself, surely he can bring to you the beautiful Sea Maiden."

"Boris Threeson," the tsar said, "you have served me well so far. You have brought me the feather of the Phoenix and you have brought me the Phoenix itself. Now you must bring me the beautiful Sea Maiden. If you do not, I swear by my throne that you will die."

Boris Threeson returned to the stable, where he hung his head and sobbed loudly.

"Why do you weep?" asked the foal.

"How should I not weep?" said Boris Threeson. "The tsar has now given me a task that the two of us together cannot accomplish."

"What is the task?" asked the foal.

"I am to bring him the beautiful Sea Maiden, or I will die," said Boris Threeson.

"I told you not to take the feather of the Phoenix," said the foal. "Now you regret it. But do not despair. We may be able to do something yet. Ask the tsar for a basketful of mirrors and one thousand dresses in trunks."

The mirrors and dresses were taken to the sea, where Boris Threeson followed the orders of the foal. He stood the mirrors up in the sand and spread the gowns over the trunks. Then they hid and waited.

When she saw the activity on the beach, Nastasia the beautiful Sea Maiden came to see what was happening. Spying the mirrors and the gowns, she came out of the sea and began trying them on.

Nastasia the Sea Maiden tried on each gown and admired herself in a mirror with each change. She was so busy with the gowns that Boris Threeson was able to walk right up to her and grab her by the arm before she even knew he was there.

"Oh, please!" she cried. "Let me go! I will give you my ring if you let me go. It will bring you much happiness."

Boris Threeson would not release her and, in despair, she tore off her pearl necklace and scattered it into the sea. Boris Threeson took her to the tsar, who was delighted and rewarded Boris Threeson generously.

One day much later, Nastasia the Sea Maiden sighed to the tsar, "Oh how I wish I had my pearls to wear again."

The tsar summoned Boris Threeson and said to him: "You have brought me a feather of the Phoenix, you have brought me the Phoenix itself and you have brought me the beautiful Sea Maiden. Now you must bring me her pearl necklace from the sea. If you do not, I swear by my throne that you will die."

Boris Threeson returned to the stable and wept. The foal came to him and said, "Why do you weep, Boris Threeson?"

"How should I not weep? The tsar has given me an order that we cannot fulfil."

"What is the order?" asked the foal.

"I am to go to the sea and retrieve the pearl necklace that Nastasia the Sea Maiden threw into the waves."

"Once more, you regret picking up the feather of the Phoenix! Well, we may do this thing yet. Ask the tsar for one hundred barrels of meat and one hundred helpers."

The tsar supplied the meat and the helpers and Boris Threeson followed the instructions of the foal. They spread the meat along the seashore and the helpers were told to grab all the crabs that came out of the sea to eat. Boris Threeson ran back and forth, inspecting each crab, searching for the one the foal had told him was the tsar of the crabs.

When he had seized the palest crab of them all, Boris Threeson held him aloft and showed him to the other crabs.

"That is our tsar!" cried the crabs. "Oh, please release our tsar, and we will do whatever you wish!"

"Bring me the pearls from the necklace that Nastasia the Sea Maiden scattered into the waves," said Boris Threeson. "Then I will release your tsar."

The crabs scuttled back into the sea and soon returned with one pearl each. Quickly they had all of the pearls. Boris Threeson was about to release the tsar of the crabs when the foal cried, "Wait! There is one pearl missing!"

The crabs scuttled back into the sea. They searched all the nooks and crevices of the rocks, until they cornered a large carp that had swallowed the last pearl. The crabs forced the carp onto the beach, where Boris Threeson cut him open and found the last pearl. He then released the tsar of the crabs.

Boris Threeson took the pearls to the tsar, who was properly pleased. Nastasia the Sea Maiden, however, told the tsar to give Boris Threeson another task.

"Tell Boris Threeson to find out why the Moon once rose early and red, but now rises late and pale."

Again Boris Threeson returned to the stable and wept.

"Why do you weep?" asked the foal. "The tsar has not yet given us a task so difficult that we could not accomplish it."

Boris Threeson told him:

"We must find out why the Moon once rose early and red but now rises late and pale."

As the foal and Boris Threeson were leaving the palace grounds, the guard of the garden gate stopped them and asked, "Where are you going, Boris Threeson?"

"We are going to find the Moon to ask him why he once rose early and red but now rises late and pale."

"Please also ask why this garden once grew enough to feed the world and now grows barely enough for the guards."

"I will do so," answered Boris Threeson.

As they travelled, Boris Threeson and the foal came upon two soldiers wrapped in chains. The soldiers asked, "Where are you going?"

"We are going to find the Moon to ask him why he once rose early and red but now rises late and pale."

"Please also ask him how long we must remain wrapped in these chains."

"I will do so," answered Boris Threeson.

As they traveled, Boris Threeson and the foal saw a man and his wife running around in circles trying to catch some doves. The pair came to a stop and asked, "Where are you going, Boris Threeson?"

"We are going to find the Moon to ask him why he once rose early and red but now rises late and pale."

"Please also ask how long we must chase these doves without catching them."

"I will do so," said Boris Threeson.

As they walked, Boris Threeson and the foal came upon a woman carrying water in pails from one well to another.

"Whither away, Boris Threeson?"

"We are going to find the Moon to ask him why he once rose early and red but now rises late and pale."

"Please ask also how long I must carry this water back and forth," said the woman.

Towards evening Boris Threeson and the foal came to a hut in front of which sat an old woman warming herself before a fire.

"Where are you going, Boris Threeson?" asked the old woman.

"We are going to find the Moon to ask him why he once rose early and red but now rises late and pale."

"Welcome, Boris Threeson," said the old woman. "I am the Mother of the Moon. Come and sit down."

Boris Threeson told her his story. "I must find out from the Moon why he once rose early and red and now rises late and pale. I also promised to find out why the garden which once fed the world now barely feeds its guards, how long the soldiers must wear their chains, how long the man and his wife must chase the doves, and how long the woman must carry the water from one well to the other."

The Mother of the Moon nodded. She gave Boris Threeson and the foal food to eat and water to drink. When the Moon was about to come home, she hid Boris Threeson and the foal in the closet.

In the morning, over breakfast the Mother of the Moon said, "I had some interesting dreams last night."

"What did you dream, Mother?"

"I dreamt that there is a garden that once fed the world but now produces barely enough to feed its guards."

"I know that garden, Mother. Thieves have buried some stolen money in the garden. If the money were dug up and removed, the garden would flourish as before."

"I also dreamt of two soldiers in chains."

"I also know of those soldiers," said the Moon. "If they were to take the money from the garden and give it to the poor, their chains would fall away."

"I dreamt also of a husband and wife chasing but not catching some doves."

"When those two were young they committed a foul deed. Now they will be chasing the doves for eternity."

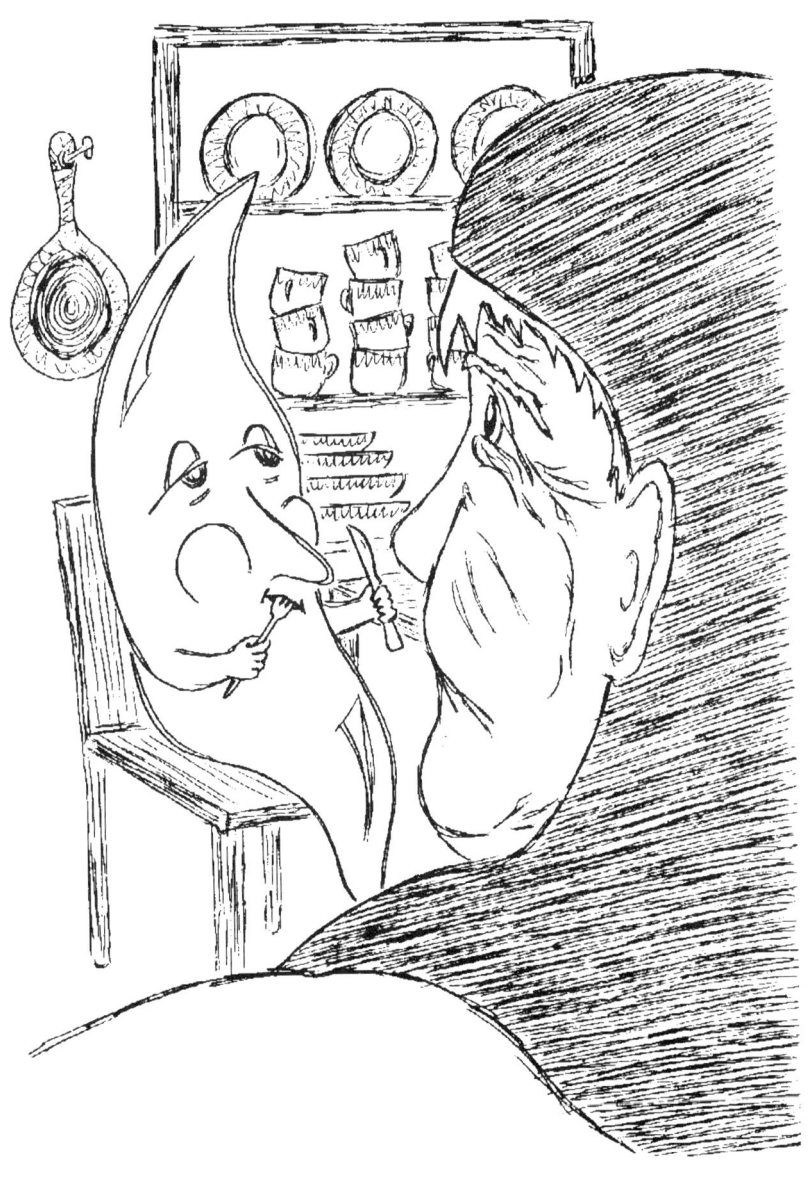

"Another dream was about a woman carrying water from one well to another."

"She will carry water forever, because she gave too much to one of her children and not enough to the other, who withered and died."

"My last dream was that you once rose early and red, but now rise late and pale."

"That is true," said the Moon. "When Nastasia the Sea Maiden lived in the sea, I rose early to gaze at her, and in the face of such beauty I turned red. Now that she is no longer in the sea, I have no desire to rise early, and I am always pale."

The Moon was ready to leave, but he felt that his mother might want to discuss her dreams further, so he wrote the answers to her questions on a piece of paper, which he gave to her. He then disappeared.

After their breakfast, the Mother of the Moon gave the paper to Boris Threeson, and he departed with the foal.

They soon came to the woman who was carrying water. "Did you ask the Moon about me?" she inquired.

"Yes, and you will be carrying water forever, because you gave too much to one of your children and not enough to the other."

"Oh," said the woman. "That is true. And now I must suffer for it. But at least I know that I will be doing this forever. I will no longer hurry; I will take my time at it."

Later, the husband and wife who were chasing the doves asked, "What have you found out about us?"

"The Moon said you committed a foul deed when you were young, and now you will chase the doves forever."

"In that case, we will not run any more. We will take our time, and perhaps one day they will come to us."

Arriving at the two soldiers in chains, Boris Threeson said, "There is some stolen money buried in a garden. If you dig up that money and give it to the poor, you will be free."

The two soldiers promised to do so, and their chains fell away. They walked on with Boris Threeson and the foal.

At the garden Boris Threeson said to the guard, "These two soldiers will dig up the stolen money that is buried here and give it to the poor. Then the garden will once more grow and bloom as before."

Finally returning to the palace, Boris Threeson told the tsar all that had happened, and gave him the note the Moon had written.

The tsar was mightily pleased with what Boris Threeson had accomplished. He rewarded Boris Threeson with half his kingdom, and from then on they lived together as brothers.

The Daughter of the Flower Queen

A young prince was riding one day through a meadow that stretched for miles when he came to a deep ditch. He was turning aside to avoid it when he heard the sound of someone crying. He dismounted and, to his astonishment, found an old woman in the ditch, who begged him to help her. The prince bent down and lifted her out of the ditch, asking at the same time how she came there.

"My son," answered the old woman, "I am very poor. Just after midnight I set out for the town to sell my eggs in the market in the morning. But I lost my way in the dark and fell into this deep ditch, where I might have remained forever but for your kindness."

The prince said, "You can hardly walk. Get on my horse and I will take you home. Where do you live?"

"At the edge of the forest in the little hut you see in the distance," replied the old woman.

The prince lifted her onto his horse and soon they reached her hut, where the old woman got down. Turning to the prince, she said, "Wait a moment, and I will give you something. Would you like to have the most beautiful woman in the world for your wife?"

"Certainly I would," replied the prince.

"The most beautiful woman in the whole world is the Daughter of the Queen of the Flowers, and she has been captured by the King of the Dragons. If you wish to marry her, you must first set her free, and this I will help you to do.

"I will give you this little bell. If you ring it once, the King of the Eagles will appear; if you ring it twice, the King of the Foxes will come to you; and if you ring it three times, you will see the King of the Fishes by your side. They will help you if you are in any difficulty. Farewell, and Heaven help you in your undertaking."

She handed him the little bell, and then disappeared, hut and all, as though the earth had swallowed her up. The prince realized that he had been speaking to a good fairy. Putting the little bell carefully in his pocket he rode home and told his father what he meant to do. He was going to free the Daughter of the Flower Queen and intended to set out on the following day in search of the maid.

Next morning the prince mounted his horse. He roamed the world for a year, and he and his horse suffered from want and misery, but he had found no trace of the princess. At last one day he came to a hut, in front of which sat a very old man. The prince asked:

"Do you know where the King of the Dragons lives who keeps the Daughter of the Flower Queen prisoner?"

"No, I do not," answered the old man, "but if you go straight along this road for a year, you will reach a hut where my father lives, and possibly he will be able to tell you."

The prince thanked him and continued his journey for a whole year along the same road. At the end of it he came to a little hut, where he found a very old man. He asked him the same question and the old man answered:

"No, I do not know where the Dragon lives. But go straight along this road for a year, and you will come to a hut in which my father lives. I know he can tell you."

The prince rode on for another year and, at last, he found the third old man. He put the same question to him as he had put to his son and grandson and the old man answered:

"The King of the Dragons lives there on the mountain and he has just begun his year of sleep. For one year he is always awake and the next he sleeps. But if you wish to see the Daughter of the Flower Queen go up the second mountain. The Mother of the Dragon lives there with her children, and she has a ball every night, to which the Daughter of the Flower Queen goes regularly."

The prince went up the second mountain, where he found a castle made of gold with diamond windows. He was just going to walk in when seven Dragons rushed on him and asked him what he wanted.

The prince replied, "I have heard so much of the beauty and kindness of the Dragon Mother that I would like to enter her service."

This pleased the Dragons and the eldest said, "You may come with me, and I will take you to the Dragon Mother."

They entered the castle and walked through twelve splendid halls made of gold and diamonds. In the twelfth room they found the Dragon Mother seated on a diamond throne. She was the ugliest woman under the sun and, added to it all, she had three heads. Her appearance was a great shock to the prince, as was her voice, which was like the croaking of many ravens. She asked him:

"Why have you come here?"

The prince answered at once, "I have heard much of your beauty and kindness. I would like very much to enter your service."

"Very well," said the Dragon Mother. "First, in the morning, you must lead my mare out to the meadow and look after her for three days. If you do not bring her home safely every evening, we will eat you up."

The prince led the mare out to the meadow. No sooner had they reached the grass than she vanished. The prince sought for her in vain; at last in despair he sat down on a stone and contemplated his sad fate. As he sat lost in thought, he noticed an eagle flying over his head. He suddenly thought of his little bell and, taking it out of his pocket, he rang it once. In a moment he heard a rustling sound in the air beside him, and the King of the Eagles landed at his feet.

"I know what you want," the bird said. "You are looking for the mare of the Dragon Mother, who is galloping about in the clouds. I will catch the mare and bring her to you."

With these words the King of the Eagles flew away. Toward evening the prince heard a mighty rushing sound in the air and, looking up, he saw thousands of eagles driving the mare before them. They came to the ground at his feet and gave the mare to him. The prince rode home to the old Dragon Mother, who was full of wonder when she saw him. She said:

"You have succeeded today in looking after my mare and, as a reward, you shall come to my ball tonight." She gave him a cloak made of copper and led him to a big room where several young Dragons were dancing together. Here, too, was the Daughter of the Flower

Queen. Her dress was woven of lovely flowers and her complexion was like lilies and roses. As the prince was dancing with her he whispered:

"I have come to set you free!"

The beautiful girl said to him, "If you succeed in bringing the mare back safely the third day, ask the Dragon Mother to give you a foal of the mare as a reward."

The ball came to an end at midnight and early the next morning the prince led the mare of the Dragon Mother into the meadow. Again she vanished before his eyes. He took out his little bell and rang it twice. In a moment the King of the Foxes stood before him and said:

"I know what you want. The mare has hidden herself in a hill."

With these words the King of the Foxes disappeared. In the evening many thousands of foxes brought the mare to the prince. He rode home to the Dragon Mother, from whom he received this time a cloak of silver, and again she led him to the ballroom.

The Daughter of the Flower Queen was delighted to see him and, when they were dancing together, she whispered in his ear, "If you succeed tomorrow, wait for me with the foal in the meadow. After the ball we will fly away together."

On the third day the prince led the mare to the meadow again and once more she vanished before his eyes. Then the prince took out his little bell and rang it three times. In a moment the King of the Fishes appeared and said to him:

"I know quite well what you want me to do. I will summon all the fishes of the sea and tell them to bring you back the mare, who is hiding in a river."

Toward evening the mare was returned to him, and he led her home. The Dragon Mother said to him, "You are a brave youth, and I will make you my bodyguard. But what shall I give you as a reward?" The prince asked for a foal of the mare, which the Dragon Mother gave him at once. She also gave him a cloak made of gold, for she had fallen in love with him.

In the evening he was at the ball in his golden cloak but, before it was over, he slipped away and went straight to the stables, where he mounted his foal and rode out into the meadow to wait for the Daughter of the Flower Queen. He placed her in front of him on the foal and they flew like the wind until they reached the palace of the Flower Queen.

The Dragons saw their escape and woke their brother, the King of the Dragons. He flew into a terrible rage and determined to lay siege to the palace of the Flower Queen.

The Flower Queen caused a forest of flowers as high as the sky to grow up round her dwelling, through which no one could possibly force their way.

When the Flower Queen heard that her daughter wanted to marry the prince she said: "I give my consent to your marriage gladly, but my daughter can only stay with you in summer. In winter, when the flowers are dead and the ground is covered with snow, she must come and live with me in my palace underground."

The prince consented and led his beautiful bride home, where the wedding was held with great pomp and magnificence. The young couple lived happily till winter came, and the Daughter of the Flower Queen went home to her mother. In the summer she returned to her husband; their life of joy and happiness began again and lasted till the approach of winter. This coming and going, summer and winter, continued all their lives long and, in spite of it, they lived happily.

The Death of the Sun-Hero

Many many years ago there lived a mighty tsar whom Heaven had blessed with a clever and beautiful son. When he was only ten years old the boy was more clever than all the counsellors of the tsar and, when he was twenty, he was thought the greatest hero in the whole tsardom. His father had him clothed in golden garments which shone and sparkled in the sun and his mother gave him a white horse which never slept and which flew like the wind. All the people in the land loved him dearly and called him the Sun-Hero, for they thought his like existed nowhere under the sun.

It happened one night that both of his parents had the same extraordinary dream. They dreamed that a girl dressed in red had come to them and said: "If you wish that your son might really become the Sun-Hero in deed and not only in name, let him go out into the wide world and search for the Tree of the Sun. When he has found it, let him pluck a golden apple and return home with it."

When the tsar and tsarina related their dreams to each other, they were much amazed that they should both have dreamed exactly the same thing about their son. The tsar said to his wife, "This is clearly a sign from Heaven."

He at once bade his son set forth in search of the Tree of the Sun, from which he was to pluck a golden apple. The prince was delighted at the thought of such an adventure, and set out on his travels that very day.

For a long time he travelled through the world, and it was not until the ninety-ninth day that he found an old man who was able to tell him where the Tree of the Sun grew. He followed his directions and rode on.

After another ninety-nine days he arrived at a beautiful golden castle which stood in the middle of a vast wilderness. He knocked at the golden door, which was opened noiselessly by invisible hands.

Finding no one about, the prince rode on again and came to a great meadow where the Tree of the Sun grew. When he reached it he put out his hand to pick a golden apple. All of a sudden the tree grew higher so he could not reach its fruit. He heard someone behind him laughing. Turning around, he saw a girl in red walking toward him.

"Do you really imagine, brave son of the earth, that you can pluck an apple so easily from the Tree of the Sun?" she said. "Before you can do that, you have a difficult task before you. You must guard the tree for nine days and nine nights from the ravages of two wild black wolves. Do you think you can undertake this?"

"Yes," answered the Sun-Hero, "I will guard the Tree of the Sun for nine days and nine nights."

The girl continued: "Remember though, if you do not succeed, the Sun will kill you. Now begin your watch."

With these words the Red Girl went back to the golden castle. She had hardly left when the two black wolves appeared. The Sun-Hero beat them off with his sword and they retired, only to reappear in a very short time. The Sun-Hero chased them away once more, but he had hardly sat down to rest when they came again. This went on for seven days and seven nights when the white horse, who had never done such a thing before, turned to the Sun-Hero and said:

"Listen to what I am going to say. A fairy gave me to your mother that I might be of service to you. Let me tell you, if you go to sleep and let the wolves harm the tree, the Sun will surely kill you. The fairy put everyone in the world under a spell, to prevent their obeying the command of the Sun to take your life. But

all the same, she forgot one person, who will certainly kill you if you fall asleep and let the wolves damage the tree. So watch and keep the wolves away."

Then the Sun-Hero strove with all his might and kept the black wolves at bay and conquered his desire to sleep. On the eighth night, however, his strength failed him and he fell asleep. When he awoke a woman in black standing beside him said:

"You have fulfilled your task very badly, for you have let the two black wolves damage the Tree of the Sun. I am the mother of the Sun, and I command you to ride away from here at once. I pronounce sentence of death upon you, for you proudly let yourself be called the Sun-Hero without having done anything to deserve the name."

The youth mounted his horse sadly and rode home. The people thronged around him on his return, anxious to hear his adventures, but he told them nothing. Only to his mother did he confide what had befallen him. The old tsarina laughed, and said to her son:

"Do not worry, my child; the fairy has protected you so far, and the Sun has found no one to kill you. Cheer up and be happy."

After a time the prince forgot about his adventure and married a beautiful princess, with whom he lived very happily for a good many years.

One day when he was out hunting, he felt very thirsty and, coming to a stream, he stooped to drink from it. This caused his death, for a crab came scuttling up and, with its claw, pierced his tongue.

He was carried to his home and, as he lay on his deathbed, the black woman suddenly appeared and said:

"The Sun has, after all, found someone in this world who was not under the spell of the fairy. Take heed! A similar fate will overtake everyone who wrongfully assumes a title to which he has no right."

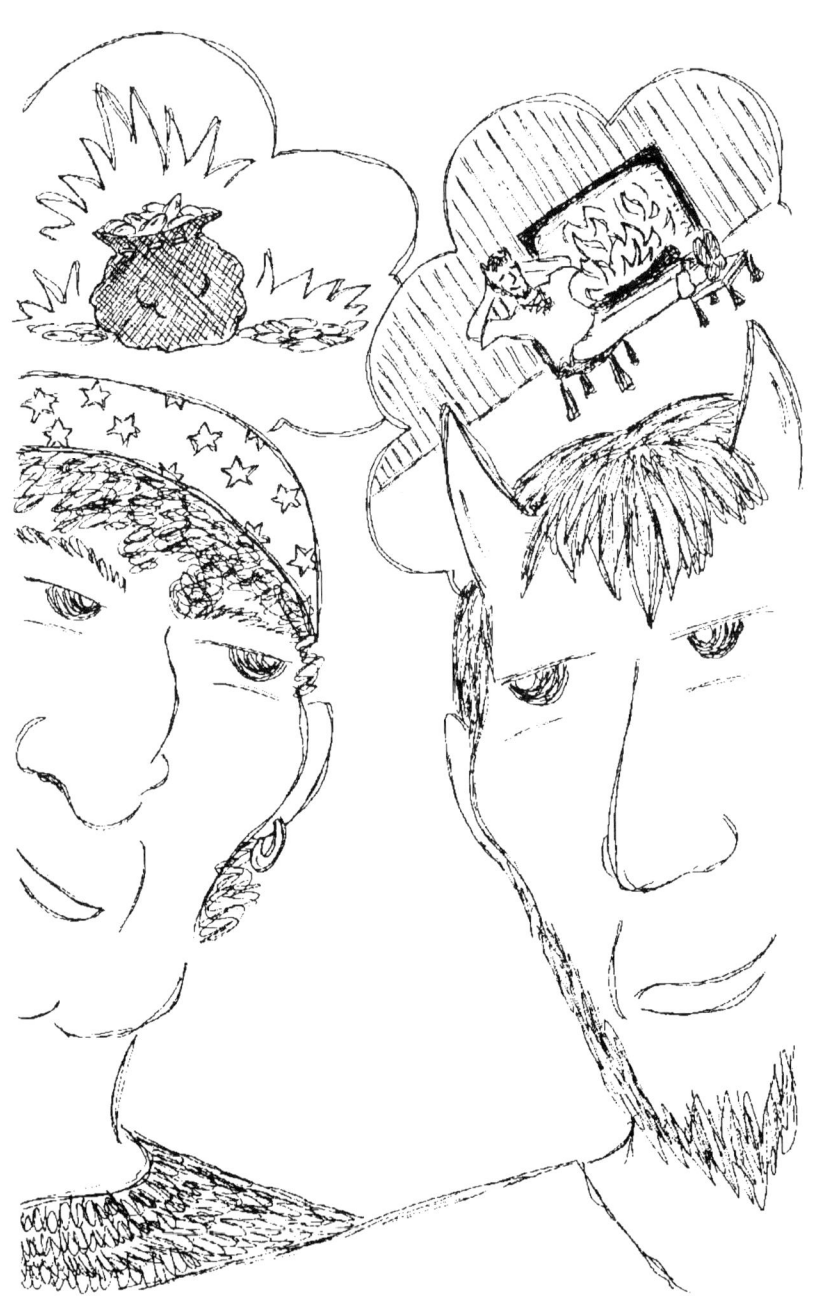

The Devil and the Gypsy

A devil hired a gypsy, saying, "I will give you a bag of gold. You will fetch my firewood and my water and make a fire under my kettle."

The devil gave the gypsy a bucket and told him to fetch water from the well. The gypsy went to the well and threw the bucket in, but he was so small he could not get the full bucket out of the water. He poured out the water so as not to lose the bucket, and sat down to think about the problem. He took a stick and began stirring around in the well.

The devil was getting tired of waiting for his water so he went to the well and saw the gypsy stirring with the stick. "What is this you are doing?" he asked when he saw what was going on.

"I was going to dig out the well and take it to your house so that I would not have to carry the water so far every day."

The devil stared at the gypsy in disbelief. "I want only a bucket full, not the whole well!" he said. He took the bucket from the gypsy, threw it into the well, drew a full bucket and carried it home. Then he sent the gypsy to get some firewood.

The gypsy went off to get the wood, but it began to rain. As he was getting lazy and unwilling to stoop to pick up the wood, he began again to think of a way to fool the devil.

The gypsy took a long rope, tied it to a tree and began to walk around the other trees, waiting for the devil. When the devil finally arrived, he asked, "What are you doing? Where is my firewood?"

The gypsy said, "What am I doing? I am bringing you wood. I am going to bring you the whole forest at once."

The devil shook his head. "I want only enough for the fire tonight, not the whole forest!" He picked up an armload of wood and headed home, thinking about the gypsy.

The devil could make no sense out of his thoughts, so he went to an old devil for advice. "I have this gypsy working for me, and he is a real bother. I think he is always tricking me. Should I kill him?"

The old devil immediately said, "Oh yes. If that is the case, then that would be the best thing to do. When he is asleep just beat him until he is no more."

The devil returned to his home, where he found the gypsy warming himself at the fire. He said nothing to the gypsy, but the gypsy could tell that there was something amiss. He did not trust the devil at all.

That night the gypsy put his fur coat on the bench where he usually slept and hid in a corner. When all was quiet the devil crept up to the bench with a large club and began to beat the fur coat for all he was worth.

After the devil finished the beating and went back to his bed, the gypsy sneaked back to his bench, put on his fur coat and began rolling around. The devil, hearing the noise, said, "Who is there? What are you doing?"

"I was bitten by a flea," said the gypsy, "and it itches."

The devil went back to the old devil for more advice. "I beat the gypsy till my club was splintered, and the gypsy thought it was only a flea. He is much stronger than I thought. What shall I do now?"

"If that is the case, you must pay him off and be rid of him," was the reply.

The devil went home, paid off the gypsy and sent him on his way with a bag of gold. After a short time, he thought to himself, "I wish I still had that bag of gold. I liked having it. I certainly got nothing for it."

He returned to the old devil to ask his advice once more.

The old devil suggested that he have a contest with the gypsy. "Whoever can kick a stone the hardest so that it makes the most noise will be the winner of the bag of gold."

The devil ran after the gypsy and told him they would have a contest to see who would have the bag of gold. "We will kick stones," he said, "and whoever kicks the hardest and makes the most noise out of the stone will have the bag of gold."

The devil began kicking a stone, sending up a great racket. Hearing nothing from the gypsy, he went to see what he was doing. He found the gypsy sitting on a rock, and the rock was soaking wet. The gypsy had poured his water bottle on the rock, but told the devil, "I do not wish to make a great noise. I only wish to kick the stone as hard as I can. Each time I kick it very hard, water squirts out of it."

The devil could not kick his stone that hard, so he again went to the old devil. "Propose another contest. Take a big heavy club, and whoever throws it the highest will have the gold."

The devil returned to the gypsy, explained the contest and threw his club straight up in the air. After a time the club fell to earth and it was the turn of the gypsy.

"This is a small enough club," he said. "I have two brothers in the clouds who are blacksmiths and they would like to have it for a hammer handle. I will just throw it to them and they can have it."

"No," said the devil. "That is my best club. You had better not do that."

This time the old devil suggested a foot race. The gypsy, when he heard the new contest, said, "I really should have nothing further to do with you. You have just been wasting my time. There is my son going by; you can race with him." The gypsy pointed to a passing rabbit. As soon as the devil started after the rabbit, it took off and was miles away before the devil even got close to him.

Beaten again, the devil went to the old devil, who this time advised: "You must wrestle with this gypsy. Surely you are stronger than a mere human being."

The devil went to the gypsy and said, "We must have a wrestling match. The winner will have the gold."

The gypsy replied: "I would probably hurt you if we were to do that. I will give you a chance, though, and let you wrestle with my father instead. He is so old that we keep him in a cave, where we feed him and he lives alone."

The devil agreed and the gypsy led the devil to a cave where a bear lived. The devil entered the cave and was lucky to escape alive.

Returning to the old devil, the young devil told his story and asked for some less dangerous advice. This time the old devil recommended a whistling contest. Whoever whistled the loudest would have the gold.

The gypsy agreed to the contest, but told the devil to cover his eyes and ears. "I will whistle so loud that you will go blind and deaf."

The devil covered his eyes and ears and the gypsy took the club and struck the devil squarely on the back of his head. "Stop whistling!" cried the devil. "You win! I will not bother you any more."

And he left the gypsy in peace.

The Giants and the Herdboy

There once was a boy who had no mother and no father. To live, he watched the sheep of a great lord. Day and night he was in the open fields, and only when it was stormy did he take refuge in a little hut on the edge of the forest.

One night when he was sitting on the grass beside his flocks, he heard the sound of crying. He rose and followed the direction of the noise. To his dismay and astonishment he found a giant lying at the entrance of the wood; he was about to run off as fast as his legs could carry him, when the giant called out:

"Fear not; I will not harm you. On the contrary, I will reward you handsomely if you will bind up my foot. I hurt it when I was trying to uproot an oak tree."

The herdboy took off his shirt and bound up the wounded foot with it. The giant rose and said very kindly and politely:

"Now come and I will reward you. We are going to celebrate a marriage today and, I promise you, we shall have plenty of fun. Come and enjoy yourself but, in order that my brothers and sisters may not see you, put this band around your waist and then you will be invisible to everyone."

With these words he handed the herdboy a belt and, walking in front, he led him to a fountain where hundreds of giants and giantesses were holding a wedding celebration.

They danced and played games till midnight, when one of the giantesses tore up a tree by its roots. All the giants and giantesses became so thin that they disappeared through the hole made by the uprooting of the tree. The wounded giant remained to the last and called:

"Herdboy, where are you?"

"Here I am, close to you," was the reply.

"Touch me," said the giant, "so that you may come underground with us."

The herdboy did as he was told and, before he could have believed it possible, found himself in a great hall, where even the walls were made of pure gold. To his astonishment he saw that the hall was furnished with the tables and chairs that belonged to his master, the wealthy lord.

The company began to eat and drink. The banquet was a gorgeous affair, and the poor youth fell to and ate and drank heartily. When

he had eaten as much as he could stuff into himself he said to himself:

"Why should I not put a loaf of bread in my pocket? I shall be glad of it tomorrow."

He seized a loaf when no one was looking and stowed it away under his tunic. No sooner had he done so than the wounded giant limped up to him and whispered softly:

"Herdboy, where are you?"

"Here I am," replied the youth.

"Hold onto me," said the giant, "so that I may lead you up above again."

The herdboy held onto the giant and in a few moments he found himself on the earth once more, but the giant had vanished. The herdboy returned to his sheep and took off the invisible belt which he hid carefully in his bag.

The next morning the lad felt hungry and thought he would cut off a piece of the loaf he had carried away from the wedding feast and eat it. Although he tried with all his might, he could not cut off the smallest piece.

In despair and hunger, the poor fellow bit the loaf, and what was his astonishment when a piece of gold fell out of his mouth and rolled at his feet! He bit the bread a second and a third time and, each time, a piece of gold fell out of his mouth but the loaf remained whole.

The herdboy was delighted over his stroke of good fortune. Hiding the magic loaf in his bag, he hurried off to the nearest village to buy himself something to eat, and then he returned to his sheep.

The lord whose sheep the herdboy looked after had a very lovely daughter who always smiled and nodded to the youth when she walked with her father in his fields. For a long time the herdboy had made up his mind to prepare a surprise for this beautiful creature on her birthday.

When the day arrived he put on his invisible belt, took a sack of gold pieces with him and, slipping into her room in the middle of the night, he placed the bag beside her bed and returned to his sheep. The joy of the girl was great, and so was that of her parents, next day when they found the sack of gold pieces.

The herdboy was so pleased to think what pleasure he had given that the next night he put another bag of gold beside the bed of the girl. This he did for seven nights, and the girl and her parents thought that it must be a good fairy who brought the gold. One night, however, they determined to hide and see from their hiding place who really left the gold beside the bed of their daughter.

On the eighth night a fearful storm of wind and rain came on while the herdboy was on his way to take the beautiful girl another sack of gold. He noticed, just as he reached the house of his master, that he had forgotten the belt that made him invisible. He did not like the idea of going back to his hut in the wind and wet, so he stepped just as he was into the room of the girl. He put the sack of gold beside her and was turning to leave the room, when his master confronted him and said:

"You young rogue, so you were going to steal the gold that a good fairy brings every night, were you?"

The herdboy was so taken aback that he stood trembling before him, and did not dare to explain his presence. Then his master spoke:

"As you have hitherto always behaved well in my service I will not send you to prison. But leave your place instantly and never let me see your face again."

The herdboy went back to his hut and, taking his loaf and belt with him, went to the nearest town. There he bought himself some fine clothes and a beautiful coach with four horses, hired two servants, and drove back to his master.

How astonished the master was to see his herdboy returning to him in this manner! The youth told him of the piece of good luck that had befallen him and asked him for the hand of his beautiful daughter. This was readily granted, and the two lived in peace and happiness to the end of their days.

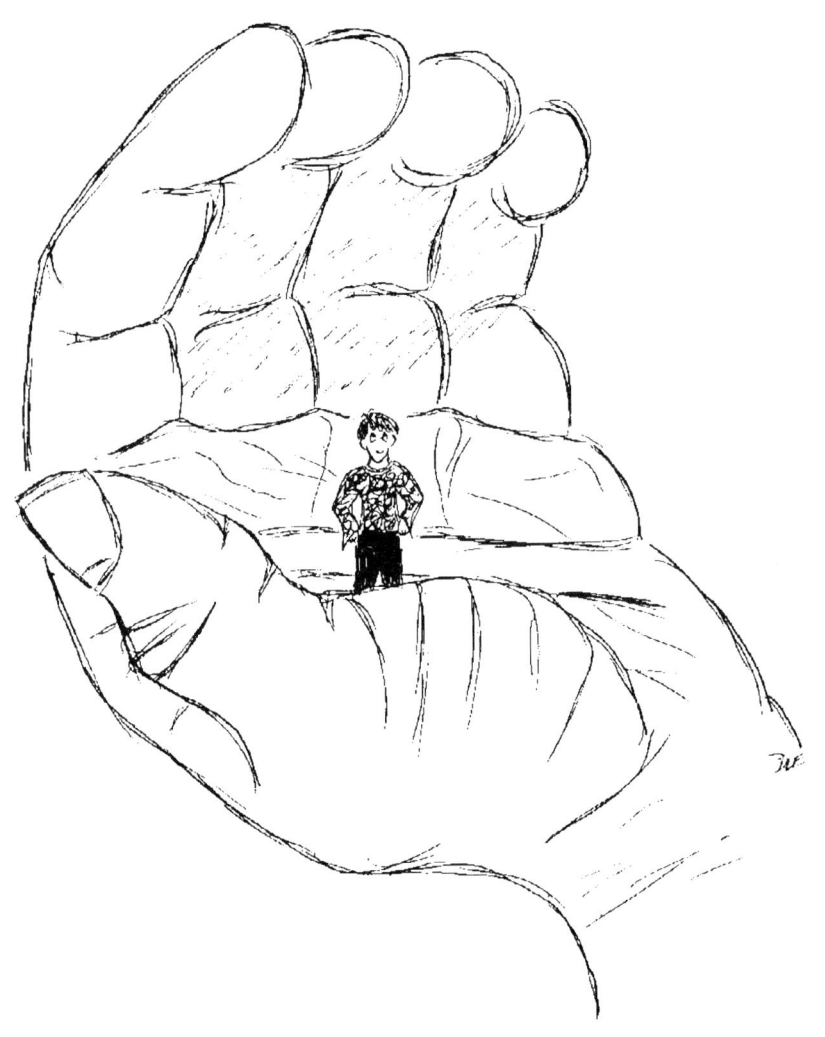

The Hazlenut Child

There was once a couple who had no children. They longed for someone to share their lives with and to whom they could leave their home. They prayed every day for a child, even if it were no bigger than a hazlenut.

One evening a little old woman came by their house and stopped to talk with them.

"Good health to you," she said. "I am weary with travel; have you a space where I could rest for the night?"

"Most assuredly, Baba," they replied. "Please come in and have some supper with us, and then we will find you a bed. In the morning we will have breakfast, and we will give you some lunch for the road."

In the morning, as she was leaving, the old woman said to the couple:

"I thank you for your hospitality. Now tell me, what is your fondest wish?"

"We long for a child, even if he is no larger than a hazlenut," was the answer.

"It shall be so," said the old woman, and she was gone.

"I wonder," said the man, "if that was a good fairy who visited us."

She must indeed have been so, for at last their prayer was heard and they had a child the size of a hazlenut, who never grew at all. The parents were devoted to the little creature and nursed and tended him carefully. Their tiny son was as clever as could be, and so sensible that all the neighbors marvelled over the wise things he said and did.

When the hazlenut child was fifteen years old, he was sitting one day in an eggshell on the table.

His mother turned to him and said:

"You are now fifteen years old. What do you wish to do with your life?"

"I intend to be a messenger," answered the hazlenut child.

"What an idea!" his mother burst out, laughing. "Why, your tiny feet would take a week to go the distance an ordinary person could cover in a minute!"

"Still, I mean to be a messenger. Send me somewhere with a message and you will see that I shall be back in next to no time."

"Very well, go to your aunt in the next village and fetch me a comb."

The hazlenut child jumped quickly out of the eggshell and ran into the street. There he found a man on horseback who was setting out for the next village. He crept up the leg of the horse, sat down under the saddle, and then began to pinch the horse. The horse plunged and reared and then set off at a fast gallop, in spite of the efforts of the rider to stop it.

When they reached the village, the hazlenut child stopped pinching, and the poor tired horse pursued its way at the pace of a snail. The hazlenut child took advantage of this and crept down the leg of the horse. He ran to his aunt and asked her for a comb. On the way home he met another rider and did the return journey in exactly the same way.

When he handed his mother the comb she was amazed, and asked him:

"How did you manage to go there and back so quickly?"

"Ah! You see, Mother, I was quite right."

His father had a horse which he often used to take out into the fields to graze. One day he took the hazlenut child with him. At midday the father said to his small son:

"Stay here and look after the horse. I must go home and give your mother a message, but I shall be back soon."

When the father had gone, a robber passed by and saw the horse grazing without anyone watching it for, of course, he could not see the hazlenut child. The robber mounted the horse and rode away. The hazlenut child, however, climbed up the tail of the horse, hid in its ear and talked to it so that it paid no attention to the robber but went straight home. The horse ran so fast that the robber was afraid to jump off.

The father was astonished when he saw a stranger riding his horse, but the hazlenut child climbed down quickly and told him what had happened, and the robber was arrested.

One autumn when the hazlenut child was twenty years old he said to his parents:

"Farewell, my dear Father and Mother. I am going out into the world, and as soon as I have become rich I will return to you."

The parents laughed at the words of the little man, and did not believe him. In the evening the hazlenut child crept onto the roof, where some storks had built their nest. The storks were fast asleep and he climbed onto the back of the father stork and bound himself by a cord to one of its wings. Then he crept among its downy feathers and fell asleep.

Winter was coming, and the storks flew south next morning. The hazlenut child flew through the air on the back of the stork. In this way he reached the country of the southern people, where the storks took up their abode.

When the people of the southern country saw the hazlenut child they were much astonished, and took him with the stork to present to the king of the country.

The king was delighted with the little creature and kept him always beside him. Soon the king grew so fond of him that he gave him a diamond that was four times as big as he was.

The hazlenut child fastened the diamond firmly under the neck of his stork with a ribbon. When he saw the storks were getting ready for their northern flight, he mounted the bird and away they went, getting nearer home every minute.

At length they came to their village, where the stork landed on the house of the hazlenut child. He undid the ribbon from the neck of the stork and the diamond fell to the ground. He covered it with sand and stones and then ran to get his parents, so that they might carry the treasure home. He himself was not able to lift the great diamond.

The parents were greatly pleased to have their son with them once more, and wept over his safe arrival. They then went to retrieve the diamond, and were once more greatly pleased.

The hazlenut child and his parents lived together in happiness and prosperity for the rest of their lives.

Ivan Invisible

Once a poor peasant woman was a servant in the home of the boyar, who had a son the same age as her son. As a result, the two boys grew up together and were like brothers when they were children.

As they grew older, however, the son of the boyar became more and more like his father. He grew to have nothing but contempt for his former playmate. He took to ridiculing him and debasing him whenever he could. Perhaps he was trying to make up for being friendly towards the son of a peasant when he was young and did not know any better.

One day, the son of the boyar, feeling particularly nasty, called the son of the peasant to him and ordered him: "Bring to me the invisible Ivan."

The poor peasant did not know what to do. He went into the deepest, darkest forest where he had never been before, and thought to lose himself there. Surely, this was preferable to the misery the son of the boyar would subject him to.

In the middle of the forest was a small clearing and, in the middle of the clearing, the lad saw a small hut. As there was no one about, he went inside.

Suddenly, he heard someone coming, and he hid under the bed. The door opened, and he heard the voice of an old man say, "Ivan Invisible, serve up!"

There were scuffling noises and other sounds the lad could not understand, and soon he heard the unmistakable sounds of the old man eating and drinking.

After a long while, the boy heard the old man say, "Ivan Invisible, take it away!" There was a slight sound, and then silence. Then he heard the door opening and closing.

Coming out from under the bed, the boy saw that he was again alone. He carefully opened the door and looked outside, but the old man had disappeared.

"Will it work for me?" he thought, and then aloud he said, "Ivan Invisible, serve up!"

In a flash, a table appeared, loaded with food and drink of every sort. The boy was amazed, and said, "Ivan Invisible, come and help me with this meal. This is more food than twelve people could eat."

"Nobody has ever asked me to eat with them before," said a voice.

"Well, now someone has. Come and eat."

The boy sat and ate until he could eat no more, and from a plate across the table, food was disappearing at a terrific rate.

When they were finished, the boy said, "Ivan Invisible, take it away!" and everything vanished instantly.

"Ivan Invisible, are you still here?"

"Yes, I am here."

"How is it that nobody ever asked you to dinner before?"

"I do not know. Perhaps it is because people do not eat with their servants."

"Are you tired of your old master, then?"

"Yes, I am."

"Well, will you come with me?"

"Oh yes, most eagerly!"

"Good. Let us go, then."

After they had walked some distance, the boy asked, "Are you still here, Ivan Invisible?"

"Oh yes, I am right here. Fear not; I will not run away from you."

As they walked, they could hear the sound of wood being chopped furiously. They came to a clearing and were amazed to see a house being built, not by men, but by an axe. The axe flew around chopping down trees, hewing the wood, and carrying the timbers to the house, where it pounded them in place.

Ivan Invisible exclaimed, "This is a remarkable axe! Master, you should trade me for that axe; then, when you call me later, I will come to you."

An old man stood on the edge of the clearing, watching the axe build his house. The boy approached him and said, "I like your axe. I will trade you Ivan Invisible for it."

"Ivan Invisible? Who is that?" asked the old man.

"Watch," said the lad. "Ivan Invisible, serve up!"

A table appeared, groaning with food, and the old man set to with a great hunger. When he had eaten his fill, he said, "This is good, this Ivan Invisible. I will trade you my axe. To make it go, you say, 'Axe, build!' and to stop it you say, 'Axe, stop!'"

The boy said, "Ivan Invisible, take it away!" and the table was gone. The old man said, "Ivan Invisible, serve up!" and the food reappeared. The old man ate again, and the boy took the axe and departed.

After walking a while, the boy said, "Ivan Invisible, are you here?"

"Yes, I am here."

Along the way, they met an old man. He was walking but, behind him, a large wooden club was hopping along.

"My dear man, what is that you have there?" asked the boy.

"That is my club," replied the old man. "Club, hit that oak tree!" The club immediately flew to a large tree, which it began to hit over and over until the tree fell down. Then the old man said, "Club, stop!" and the club returned to him.

The boy said, "Ivan Invisible, serve up!" and in front of the old man a table covered with food and drink appeared. They sat and ate until they could eat no more, and the lad said, "Ivan Invisible, take it away!"

"This Ivan Invisible," said the old man. "I will trade you my club for him."

Ivan Invisible whispered into the ear of his master, and the boy said aloud to the man, "Yes, I will do that."

The old man said, "Ivan Invisible, serve up!" and began eating again, and the boy went on his way, the club following.

After a while, he called, "Ivan Invisible, are you here?"

"Yes, I am here."

Arriving at the city, the boy went to an inn, where he said, "Ivan Invisible, serve up." Instantly, a table with food appeared. A soldier drinking at the inn saw this and came to help the boy eat his meal.

"Watch this," said the soldier to the boy. "Switches, show us what you can do!" With a *whisshh*, three willow switches appeared and danced and whistled about their ears.

"Will you trade me your Ivan Invisible for these wonderful switches?" asked the soldier.

Again, Ivan Invisible whispered in his ear, and the boy said, "Yes. I will trade."

The boy left the city. Once in the country, he asked, "Ivan Invisible, are you here?"

"Yes, I am here."

The boy went home and appeared before his boyar, who was entertaining guests. The boyar shouted to his servants, "Grab that filthy peasant and put him in chains!"

The boy said, "Club, hit these servants!"

The club flew after the servants and chased them all over the yard, beating them and frightening them out of their wits.

The boy said, "Switches, let us teach the boyar some manners!" and the switches flew to the boyar and whipped him until he ran and hid in his bedchamber. The boy said, "Switches, teach the son of the boyar some manners, too!" and the switches immediately began chasing the son around the yard.

"If you bother me again, you will get more of the same," said the boy, and he took his friends and went home.

Once home, the boy found a spot to build himself a house. "Axe, build," he said, and the axe built him a comfortable house.

The boy and his friends all moved in and lived together in peace and harmony.

The Lazy Wolf

Once upon a time there lived a very lazy wolf. While his brother wolves were busy hunting, he merely pretended. One day the pack leader caught him having a snooze.

"You never do anything good. Never come to us for food again," the leader snarled.

After a week of hunting by himself, the lazy wolf was so thin that his sides shook hands with his backbone. He went to the home of a peasant to ask for something to eat.

"Have pity on me," he whined. "Give me something to eat or I shall die of hunger."

"What would you like?" the surprised peasant asked. He did not like the wolf.

"Just anything will do," said the wolf, his eyes brimming with tears.

"Well, do you see that old mare grazing in the field by the road? Why do you not you go and eat her? She would be easy to catch."

Pleased, the wolf ran off to the meadow.

"Good morning, Mare!" he called. "Come over here! Peasant has told me to eat you."

"Who are you that you want to eat me?" asked the mare.

"I am a wolf."

"You are lying; you are only a dog!"

"No, I am a wolf, I swear it!"

"Well, if that is true, which part of me will you eat first?"

"Your head!" said the wolf.

"My head?" said the mare. "You poor, poor dog! You do not think these things out. If you really intend to eat me, would it not be better to begin with my tail? While you are eating your way to my middle, my head will still be grazing. That way, I will keep nice and fat until you are ready for the rest of me."

"That sounds reasonable," said the wolf, and he seized the tail of the mare in his teeth. The mare kicked out at him and her hoof struck him hard across his muzzle. Then she galloped off in a cloud of dust.

The wolf hardly knew if he were dead or alive. As he rubbed his sore nose, he thought, "Fool that I am! Why did I not seize her by the throat? And I am still hungry!"

Back he went to the house of the peasant.

"Please, Peasant," he whined, "have pity on me! I am about to die of hunger."

The peasant looked astonished.

"Was the mare not enough?" he asked.

At the mention of the dinner that had escaped him, the wolf let out a great howl.

"The mare!" he yelped. "I hope they skin her alive! I hope they make leather straps out of her hide! Look how she squashed my nose!"

"Well," said the peasant, "go and eat that fat ram that you see grazing on the hilltop."

Off the wolf ran, to try again for a dinner.

"Hello, Ram," said the wolf. "Peasant has told me to eat you."

"And who are you that you want to eat me?" asked the ram.

"A wolf."

"You are lying; you are a dog."

"No, I am a wolf, I swear it!"

"Well, if that is so, how will you go about eating me?"

"Aha! I will begin with your head."

"My head?" said the ram. "Ah, you poor, poor dog! How little you know! If you really intend to eat me, you must stand at the bottom of this hill. Then, when you open your mouth wide, I will run down and jump straight in."

"That sounds reasonable," said the wolf. He stood at the bottom of the hill and opened his jaws so wide you could see right down his throat. The ram ran straight at him. He butted the wolf with his head and the poor wolf rolled across the field.

He sat up and began to cry.

"Fool that I am," he sobbed. "Where are my wits? Who has ever heard of living meat jumping into your mouth by itself?"

He thought about this for a time, then went back to the house of the peasant.

"Please," he said, "have pity on me! Give me something to eat or I shall die of hunger."

By this time the peasant had lost his patience with the wolf.

"A fine eater you are! You want your food to jump right down your throat!"

At these words of truth, the wolf raised his nose and sent out a mournful howl.

"Oh, there is no use trying to talk sense into you," the peasant said. "Down the road an old woman lost a piece of bacon on her way back from the market. The bacon will surely be yours. It cannot run away."

The wolf went down the road and there was the bacon, just as the peasant had told him. His mouth watered as he sniffed it.

"This is all very well," he said to himself, "but this bacon is sure to be salty. That will make me thirsty. If I am to enjoy it, I had better find a drink of water before I eat it."

The wolf went off to the river to drink.

In the meantime, the old woman missed her bacon. She came back to where it lay on the road, picked it up and went home.

When the wolf came back and saw that the bacon was gone, he sat down and howled.

"Fool that I am!" he said. "Where are my wits? Who has heard of anyone drinking before they eat?"

The more he thought about the bacon, the hungrier he became. So, once again, he knocked at the door of the peasant.

"Please, Peasant," he said, "have pity on me! Give me something to eat or it will be the end of me."

The peasant looked at him sternly. "What is to be done with the likes of you? You make me sick with your begging."

But the peasant had a soft heart and the wolf looked more dead than alive.

"There is a pig living in the woods near the village. Go and eat her. And do not bother me again!"

Off the wolf went again, and he soon found the pig.

"Hello, Pig," he said, "Peasant has told me to eat you."

"Who are you that you want to eat me?" asked the pig.

"I am a wolf."

"You are lying; you are a dog."

"No, I am a wolf, I swear it!"

"Are times so bad that wolves cannot get food for themselves nowadays?"

"That is right," said the wolf.

"If that is so," said the pig, "then get on my back and I will take you to the village. They are choosing the elders there today, so perhaps they will choose you!"

"Very well, let us go!"

The wolf climbed up on the back of the pig and soon they came to the village. Entering the village, the pig began to squeal so loudly that the wolf became uneasy.

"What on earth are you squealing like that for?" he asked.

"I am calling the villagers together so that they can choose you for their elder."

Sure enough, the villagers heard the pig and came running up. They carried pokers, pitchforks, shovels — whatever they could get their hands on. The sight of all the people amazed the wolf.

"Why are so many people running here?" he asked in a whisper.

"To see you," the pig replied.

The villagers surrounded the wolf and began to beat him. He forgot his hunger. He forgot to be lazy. He rushed down the road so fast he left the villagers far behind him.

Turning a corner, the wolf ran straight into a tailor who was walking toward him with a yardstick in his hand.

"I am going to eat you up," the desperate and angry wolf said.

"And who are you that you could even think of such a thing?"

"I am a wolf."

"You are lying; you are a dog."

"No, I am not a dog! I am not a dog! I am a wolf, I swear it!"

"You look small for a wolf. Here, let me measure you."

The tailor twisted the tail of the wolf round and round in his hand. Then he began to beat him with his stick, saying, "A yard in length, a yard in width!"

The frightened wolf twisted free of the tailor with all his strength. He ran as fast as his legs could carry him — not to the peasant, but straight to his own brothers, the wolves.

"Little Brothers!" he cried. "Something terrible has happened to me!"

The lazy wolf told them the story and they were so angry that they forgot to be upset with him. They all set off at a run after the tailor.

The tailor had been brave enough with one wolf but, when he saw the whole pack, he was afraid and he climbed to the top of a tree. The wolves stood around the tree and gnashed their teeth at him.

The lazy wolf said: "We will never get him this way. Here is what we must do. I shall stand here at the foot of the tree. One of you will stand on my back and someone else on his. And so on until we have reached him."

The wolves did as their lazy brother told them and climbed up on one another. The top wolf grinned up at the man in the tree.

"Well, Tailor, you had better climb down quietly. We are going to eat you up."

"Oh," said the tailor, "do have pity on me, Little Brothers, please do not eat me!"

"But we must," said the wolves, "so do not waste time."

"Wait," said the tailor. "You might at least let me take a sniff of my tobacco before I die."

The wolves waited while he sniffed his tobacco and — Achoo! — he let out a tremendous sneeze right in the face of the top wolf, who yelped in surprise.

The lazy wolf at the bottom of the ladder heard the sneeze and the yelp. He thought the tailor was beating the top wolf and saying, "A yard in length." He jumped in fright, and this sent the ladder of wolves tumbling to the ground in a heap. The frightened wolf took to his heels and the rest followed.

The tailor climbed down from the tree with a big smile on his face and went his way home, whistling happily.

The Lion in the Well

Long, long ago there lived in the middle of a large, thick forest a vicious Lion. He was so large and fearsome that he had only to roar, and all the other animals trembled and feared for their lives. When he was hunting he destroyed everyone who got in his way. He killed much more than he needed to eat, and no animal was safe from him.

The other animals, not knowing how to deal with this grave matter, called a meeting to discuss the situation. At the meeting all personal differences were set aside in order to deal with their common problem — survival.

"Listen, friends," said Bear, "Lion is killing as many of us as cross his path. He eats only one or two and the rest die for no reason. This cannot continue. I suggest we talk to him and see if he will change his ways. Otherwise, there will soon be none of us left alive."

"He will not listen to us," said Wolf. "He would be happy that his food came to him, and he would eat up all of our messengers."

"I do not think so," said Bear. "We must send the right messenger, someone he would listen to."

"You must go speak to him, Bear," said Wolf. "You are the biggest and strongest of us all. He will listen to you."

"I may be big, but I am still no match for Lion. As soon as he saw me he would think I was a threat to him, and he would kill me. You should go, Wolf. You are the most nimble of us and can stay out of his reach."

"That may be, but I am still not fast enough to escape his anger," said Wolf. "We will have to think of a way to outwit him, since we cannot fight his strength."

"Yes," cried all the animals. "But who will go? Who is wise enough to do the right thing?"

They thought of every animal in the forest. Mouse was too small, Rabbit too timid, Squirrel too silly, Deer too much to the taste of Lion, and so on. Finally, everyone was silent. Then, someone said, "Let us send Fox. She is certainly the most clever of us."

"Oh no," said Fox. "I am not that clever. Let all of us go together."

"If we do that," said Bear, "it would certainly anger Lion and then we would be no better off. Many of us would die in the effort to escape. It seems that you are chosen, Fox. If you do not agree to go, we will tear you to pieces ourselves, so you will just have to make the best of it."

"If that is the way things are, it will be the end of me no matter what I do," thought Fox. Aloud she said, "Very well. I will try my best."

"Thank you, Fox," cried all the animals. "Good luck."

As Fox was on her way to find Lion, she passed the well on the edge of the forest. It was a large round stone structure, and very deep. Fox stopped to peer into the depths of the water and, while looking at her reflection, was suddenly struck with an idea.

Fox headed straight for the den where Lion lived. There he was, basking in the sun and thinking of how many animals he would kill that day.

"Your Majesty," she began when Lion had spotted her, "please do not kill me. I have some important news for you. This morning while I was hunting in the bush, I met a large and fierce Lion who looked and sounded very much like you. He said to come and tell you that he was moving into the forest and that you had better beware."

At this the furious Lion let out a mighty roar which echoed and re-echoed through the forest. "There he is now, Your Majesty," said Fox. "He is a large Lion."

"Take me to him at once," roared Lion. "I will show him who is King of the Forest!"

Fox led Lion to the well and said, "He lives in this stone palace. If you look down you will see him, but be careful. He is mean."

Lion looked down the well and saw the face of a fierce Lion looking back at him.

"Roarrrrr!!" roared Lion and, when the echo came back to him, he became so angry that he leaped into the stone palace to kill the new Lion. Of course, there was only his reflection to fight, and the sides of the well were too steep for him to get out. After a violent struggle, the waters closed over Lion and all was peaceful in the forest once more.

The Lute Player

Once there were a tsar and tsarina who lived happily in their tsardom. The tsar practised battle with his boyars, but he grew bored and restless for the real thing. He wanted to try himself in battle and to win great fame and glory for himself and his tsardom.

He called his council and told them:

"My boyars and I are about to go on a journey. There is a cruel and evil tsar in a country far away, and we will go there to vanquish him in battle. The tsarina will rule in my stead until we return. Ministers of the crown, you are to assist the tsarina as though you were assisting me. And you, my dear, I know will take good care. You have always shared in my rule, and you have always been wise in your decisions."

Preparations were quickly made and soon the tsar rode away with his army.

The way was long and hard and the army of the tsar was tired by the time they got to the site of the battle. The evil tsar had assembled an immense army and destroyed the army of the good tsar. Many boyars were killed, and the rest, including the tsar himself, were thrown into prison.

The prisoners were treated badly by the evil tsar. They were chained together day and night and were fed very poorly.

The tsarina, meanwhile, ruled her land with such wisdom and compassion that her people prospered. However, she was worried about her husband, as she had not heard from him for three years.

One day in the prison, a rumor went around that one of the prisoners was about to be ransomed by his brother, who was a wealthy tsar in another tsardom. Our unfortunate tsar seized this opportunity to send a message to his wife, and told her:

"The tsar who has captured me is greedy, and will do anything for gold. Therefore, take all the gold in our tsardom and send it with a trusted minister to ransom me."

The tsarina was overjoyed to hear that her husband was alive, and she said to herself:

"I must free my husband as quickly as I can but, if I strip the tsardom of its wealth, he will return to an empty land. That would surely be as bad as living in a prison. If this tsar is so evil, there is nothing to stop him from seizing our messenger and holding him for ransom as well. I will go myself to this tsardom where he is imprisoned and see what I can do. I will tell nobody, as they would be certain to stop me."

The tsarina made her preparations in secret. She disguised herself as a boy, hiding her long red hair under a cap and dressing as a minstrel. She took her lute under her arm and left the castle unnoticed.

The tsarina walked along the road, feeling quite unsafe. She had no desire to travel alone, as the way was long and fraught with danger. That very day, as she entered the courtyard of an inn, she found herself in the midst of a large uproar of people who were milling about in preparation for departure.

Approaching the leader of the group, the tsarina asked:

"Whither are you travelling? Have you room for one more small soul?"

"Ho ho!" boomed the leader. "A company such as ours always has room for one more! Especially a minstrel, as we have none at the moment. You are welcome, lad."

The party revealed themselves to be merchants, bound for many lands to buy and sell goods of all descriptions. They felt safe, as they were many in number and well-armed. They were a merry lot, and they soon grew to love the tsarina and her music.

The singing and the playing of the tsarina so enchanted the merchants that, when they finally arrived at her destination and she declared her resolve to pursue her fortune in that country, they were sorry to have her leave. With many protestations of affection, they bade her farewell and good luck.

"You are welcome with our group at any time," said the leader. "We stay here three days and then return along the path by which we came. If you travel in our direction, we will gladly claim you as our own."

In the company of the merchants, the tsarina was shown into the court of the evil tsar. At the banquet that evening, she proved to be far superior in skill to any of the musicians of the country, and the tsar asked her to play for him the next day.

"Whence do you come?" asked the tsar, "and where are you going?"

"I come from afar," was the reply, "and I have far to travel. I sing and play in all the world, seeking my fortune."

"Stay some time and play for me, and I will play a part in the discovery of your fortune," promised the tsar.

"This I will do, Sire, but when the time comes for me to leave, I must follow my heart."

"Agreed," said the tsar, and the tsarina lute-player went to the palace next day. There, she played and sang her way right into the heart of not only the tsar, but also the hearts of all who heard her.

"Will you stay one more day to play for me?" asked the tsar.

"I will do so," replied the lute-player.

The next day, the tsar again asked the lute-player to return, and she said:

"I will play for you tomorrow, your Majesty. But on the next day, I must depart. My heart calls me homeward."

After the third day of music, the lute-player went to take leave of the tsar.

"You have pleased me well with your beguiling music," said the tsar. "I will give you as much gold as you can carry."

"Gold has no value for me, your Majesty," said the lute-player. "I would rather have a companion. Give me one of the prisoners from your dungeon to travel with me, and I will consider myself richly rewarded."

"Willingly I will do so," replied the tsar. "Let us go to the dungeon, and you may pick the one you want."

In the dungeon, the tsarina spotted her husband, although she had trouble to recognize him. He was thin and filthy, although he seemed to be healthy enough.

"I will take that one," said the lute-player. "I like his eyes; I feel he is kind."

The lute-player and her slave joined the group of merchants, who were enchanted with the story of how she refused gold for the sake of a companion.

The group travelled for many days, and each day was spent in merriment and good fellowship. The tsarina kept apart from her husband as much as she could, for she feared that he might recognize her and chastise her for risking herself in such a manner.

When they finally reached the border of their own land, the prisoner-slave said to the lute-player:

"Know, fair lad, that I am tsar of these lands. The story I told you of my ill-fated expedition and my capture are all true, and this is my tsardom. Come with me to the palace, and I will reward you well."

"I have no need of a reward," said the lute-player. "You are free to go with God."

"But come as my guest. I appreciate what you have done for me and my people, and wish to thank you properly. I do not look much like a tsar at this moment, but I am grateful to you."

"I will appear at the palace when I appear," replied the lute-player.

That night, as the tsar slept, the tsarina sped off on a horse and reached the palace in darkness. She entered the palace and slept in her own bed for the first time in many months.

In the morning, the lute-player put on her own clothes and shook her red hair out, becoming once more the tsarina.

Descending to the courtyard, she could hear a great cry:

"Our tsar has returned to us! Long live the tsar! Long live the tsar!"

The tsar greeted everyone, but to his wife he said:

"Did you not receive my message? You were to ransom me from the evil tsar, but instead I was rescued by a mere minstrel boy."

Before she could reply, one of his ministers came to the tsar and said:

"The day after your message arrived, the tsarina disappeared. She has only returned today. We know nothing of why she ran and hid herself, but here she is today, expecting to be taken to your heart."

The tsar was greatly saddened by this news. This was not what he had expected of his wife, the tsarina. He left her in the courtyard and went with his ministers to resume the governing of his tsardom.

The tsarina went to her chambers and once more put on the clothes of the lute-player. Again, she hid her red hair under a cap and, taking her lute, she returned to the courtyard. There, she sang one of the songs she had sung on the journey home.

The tsar heard the song and immediately recognized it.

"There!" he cried. "That is the minstrel who rescued me from the evil tsar! Bring him into the palace, and we will reward him well for what he has done."

The lute-player was brought before the tsar. There, he bowed low and, in so doing, dropped his cap upon the floor.

Standing, the lute-player shook his head so that his red hair flowed. The astounded tsar saw that the lute-player was none other than his own wife, the tsarina.

A gasp echoed through the court.

"My husband," said the tsarina, "I feared to tell you what I had done, as I feared you would be displeased with me risking my life for you. Now I will tell you all.

"I did receive your message, but thought my plan the better. I was not willing to impoverish our land while there was still a chance of rescuing you through other means. Now you have returned to a prosperous land, and your subjects welcome you eagerly."

The tsar recognized the wisdom and the courage of the tsarina and embraced her warmly. He then proclaimed a feast of celebration, and for seven days and seven nights, the entire tsardom thrilled to the music of the tsarina and her husband the tsar.

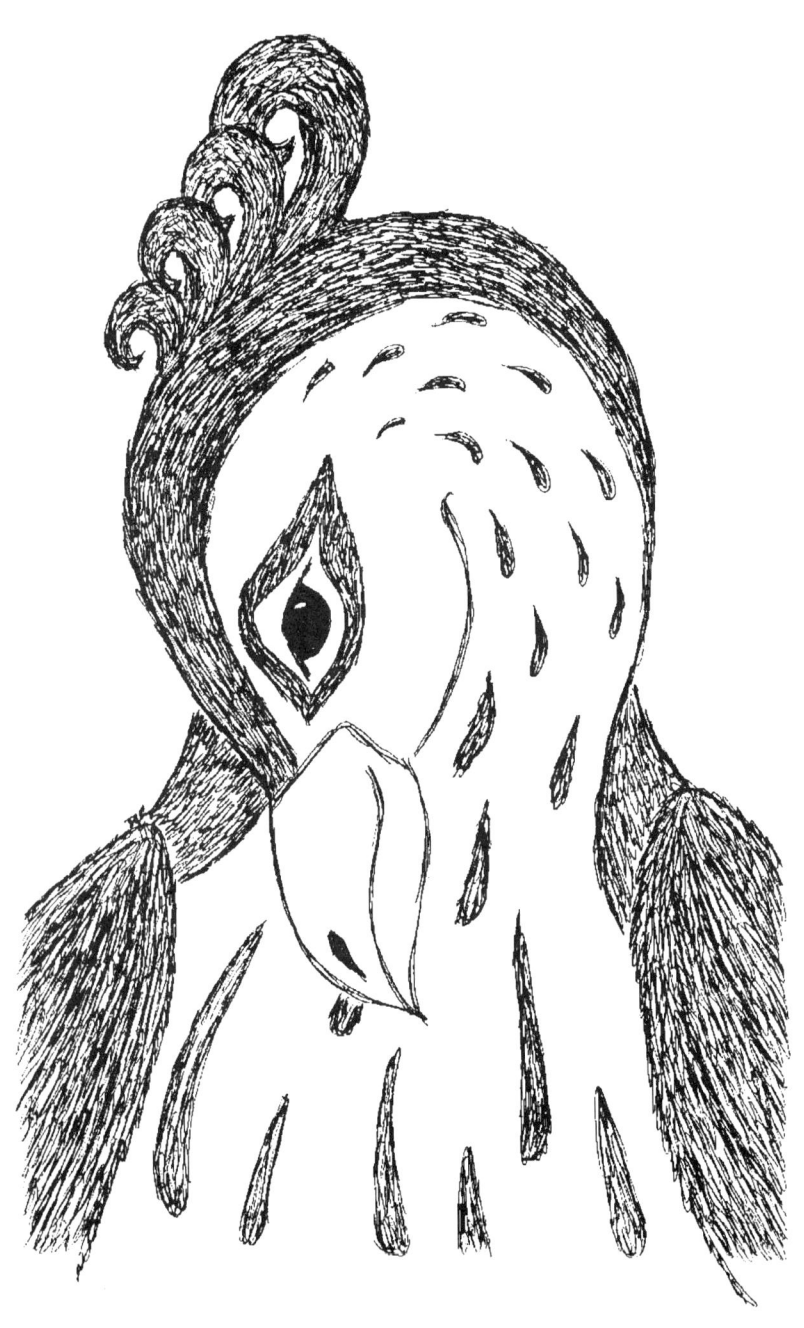

The Magic Bird

There were two brothers who lived not very far from each other. One was wealthy because he had listened to his father and married the girl his father had picked for him. The other brother was poor, because he had married for love.

The poor brother had a small piece of land, but he had nothing to sow on it. He went to his brother and said, "Brother, please give me some kind of seed that I can sow on my little bit of land."

The rich brother made all kinds of excuses; he forgot, or he did not know what kind of seed to give, or he needed it all for planting himself.

"Spring is coming soon," said the poor brother one day, "and I have nothing to sow. Please give me some seed and I will pay you back by working for you."

The rich brother took note of this and went home to confer with his wife, who was just as miserly as he was. "Here we will have a worker for next to nothing," he said. "What seed shall we give him?"

"Let us give him millet," she replied. "But I will roast it in the pich so that it will not grow. That way, he will have to come back to work for more seed and we will have cheap labor for a long time."

The poor brother sowed the millet and prayed for a good crop, but nothing grew. He went to the field day after day, but nothing came out of the earth. He worked off his debt to his brother, but the seed did not grow.

One day as the poor man was out in his field, he spotted a single millet plant that somehow had managed to sprout. He took very good care of the seedling. He watched over it, he sat by it in the field, he hoed the weeds away, he watered it with his own hat. With such good care the seedling grew like a tree. It became so large that the man was afraid someone would break it in the field, and he began to spend his nights beside the plant.

A big bird landed on the plant and began to peck at it. The man took off his jacket and hat and waved them at the bird, trying to chase the bird away.

"Go away!" he cried. "You will ruin it for me, and I have only one!"

The bird looked at the man. "You have only one plant?" he asked.

"Yes, yes! Look around you. Look how empty my field is."

"Well, in that case, I will help you," said the bird. "I will eat up this plant and then you will sit on my back and I will fly you to a place you will like to see."

The poor fellow stood there wondering at all of this. A bird that can talk, and then he has to sit on its back and fly away! What if he were to fall off?

The huge bird finished eating the millet plant and sat on the ground. The man climbed onto his back and the bird soared effortlessly into the air. They flew and flew and flew, over the mountains and over the water. They finally came to an island all made of gold, and there they landed.

"There you are," said the bird. "Get yourself some gold."

The poor fellow did not know what to do. He had no sack or anything to carry the gold. He took off his trousers and tied knots in the legs, and he took off his jacket and tied knots in the sleeves. These he filled with gold.

The bird was ready to go, and they flew off home. They flew and flew over the water, and the bird said, "I must have food. Give me something to eat or my strength will fail and we will fall into the water."

"I have nothing to feed you," said the man. "I brought nothing to eat."

"I must have something," said the bird.

The man looked around; there was nothing on the bird but the gold and him. The bird could not eat the gold, but he could eat the man. He drew his knife and cut a piece from the calf of his leg. This he fed to the bird. He tied up his leg as best he could, hoping that it would grow back in.

Finally they landed at the field of the poor man. The bird flew off, leaving the man with his gold. He managed to limp home and, after resting his leg for a few days, he began to sell off the gold, little by little.

His greedy brother came by to see how the millet was growing and, instead, he saw a cow in the yard and the house was fixed up. "What is all this, brother?" he asked. "Where did you get the money to do all this?"

At first, the man did not want to tell him. He knew what a greedy sort of person he was, and that he did not help him when he needed seed. Finally, though, he told him the story.

"One single seed grew from the grain you gave me, and it grew into a huge plant. One day a bird came and ate the plant and, in return, the bird flew me to an island of gold. That is what happened."

The rich brother hurried home and planted one millet seed. When it sprouted he took care of it and it grew to be very large. The bird came and ate up the plant and then said, "Sit on me. We are going to get gold."

The man jumped on, carrying a great load of sacks under his clothing. They flew to the golden island and the man filled all of his sacks. "Do not take too much," said the bird. "I will not be able to carry all that."

"Oh no, if you go slowly we will manage," said the man.

The bird managed to stagger into the air with the load, and they flew off. They were flying just above the water, and the bird was struggling with the weight.

"I must have something to eat," said the bird. "You have too much weight on me and, if you do not feed me something, I will not be able to carry you."

"I have nothing to feed you. Why did you not tell me before?"

"I must have food," said the bird, "and I must have it quickly!"

The man replied, "I have nothing to eat. This is your fault for not telling me! Fly on!"

The bird simply could not carry all that weight any more. He rolled over and the man with all his gold fell into the water. The bird flew on, but the greedy man was drowned.

The Man and the Priest

Once a man was walking along the road. He had walked a long way and he stopped at an inn to spend the night.

A woman answered his knock.

"We have another traveller here, a priest," said the woman. "But you can share the room."

"Wake me early in the morning, as I have a long way to go tomorrow," the man said.

The priest asked the woman not to wake him. He did not have far to go and was tired.

Next day, the woman woke the man before dawn. He dressed in the dark and hurried off into the morning. The sun came up as he walked and, looking down at himself, he saw that he had on the robe of the priest instead of his own coat.

He stopped in anger and hollered, "That stupid old woman! Now I will have to go all the way back. She woke the priest instead of me!"

The Tremendous Turnip

Dido planted a turnip in the garden.
It grew and it grew and it grew.
When the time came to pull it up, the turnip was huge.
Dido took hold of the stem.
He pulled on the stem, but the big turnip would not budge.
It was stuck fast.
"Baba!" he called. "Come and help me pull our turnip!"
Baba ran to help.
She wrapped her arms around Dido.
Baba pulled on Dido while Dido tugged on the turnip.
They pulled and they pulled, but the large turnip would not budge.
It was stuck fast.
Baba called to Mama, "Tanya, come and help us pull our turnip!"

Mama ran to hold Baba while Baba pulled Dido, and Dido pulled on the turnip with all of his might.

They pulled and they pulled and they pulled, but still the great turnip did not move.

It was stuck fast.

"Hanya! Hanya!" called Mama to her daughter. "Come and help us pull our turnip!"

Hanya ran as fast as she could.

She held on to Mama, while Mama pulled Baba, Baba pulled Dido, and Dido tugged the turnip with all his might.

They pulled and they pulled and they pulled and they pulled, but still they could not move the turnip.

The enormous turnip was stuck fast.

"Vanya! Vanya!" called Hanya to her puppy. "Come and help us pull our turnip!"

"Woof, woof!" Vanya barked loudly.

He ran and grabbed Hanya by the dress with his teeth.

He pulled Hanya, while Hanya pulled Mama, Mama pulled Baba, Baba pulled Dido, and Dido pulled the turnip with all his might.

They pulled and they pulled and they pulled and they pulled and they pulled, but still the immense turnip would not budge.

It was stuck fast.

Vanya called to Anya the kitten,

"Come and help us pull our turnip!"

"Meow, meow!" mewed Anya.

She took Vanya by the tail with her paws and hung on tight.

Anya pulled Vanya, Vanya pulled Hanya, Hanya pulled Mama, Mama pulled Baba, Baba pulled Dido, while Dido tugged and tugged with all his might.

They pulled and they pulled and they pulled and they pulled and they pulled and they pulled, but even now the massive turnip would not move.

It was stuck fast.

Manya the mouse heard all the noise.

"Squeak, squeak!" she cried and ran from her hole.

She grasped Anya by the tail.

Manya pulled Anya, Anya pulled Vanya, Vanya pulled Hanya, Hanya pulled Mama, Mama pulled Baba, and they all pulled Dido, who huffed and puffed as he tugged and tugged with all his might.

They pulled and they pulled and they pulled and they pulled and they pulled and they pulled and they pulled, but the gigantic turnip would not budge.

It was stuck just as fast as before.

Petanya the beetle came to see what was going on.

He took the tail of Manya in his claws.

Petanya pulled Manya, Manya pulled Anya, Anya pulled Vanya, Vanya pulled Hanya, Hanya pulled Mama, Mama pulled Baba, and they all pulled Dido, who tugged and tugged on the monstrous turnip.

They pulled and they pulled and they pulled and they pulled and they pulled and they pulled and they pulled and they pulled.

Suddenly, "Whoomp!"

They pulled that tremendous turnip right out of the ground!

The turnip landed on Dido; Dido fell on Baba, Baba fell on Mama, Mama fell on Hanya, Hanya fell on Vanya, Vanya fell on Anya, Anya fell on Manya, but Petanya ran away and nobody fell on him.

That night they had a tremendous turnip dinner and everyone went right to bed, including Petanya the beetle.

"How strong I am!" he thought, and he fell fast asleep.

Truth and Lies

Once there were two brothers. One was rich and one was poor. One day they were talking together, and the poor one said:

"No matter how bad things may be on this earth, it is still better to live by the truth."

"Truth? Where can you find the truth these days?" exclaimed the rich brother. "There is no truth anywhere in this world; there are only lies and deceit everywhere. No, no, we are better to stick with lies!"

"No, dear brother," insisted the poor brother. "You are wrong. Truth is better."

"Let us make a bet," said the rich one. "We will go among the people and ask the first three we meet. If they agree with you, I will give you everything I own. If they agree with me, you must give me everything you own."

"Agreed," said the poor brother, and they went down the road.

After a short time, they met a man whose wages were in his pocket.

"Good day, friend," they called.

"Good day to you, too."

"We would like to ask you something."

"So ask."

"How can you live better in this world, with the truth or with lies and deceit?"

"Oh, my dear people," answered the man. "Where can you find the truth? I worked and worked, but the master took most of the few coins I earned. If I had lied to him about how much I had earned, I would be much better off. Yes, I prefer lies."

Turning to his poor brother, the rich one said, "Well, brother. The first person has agreed with me."

This made the poor brother sad, but they walked on and soon met up with a merchant riding his horse.

"Good day to you, Sir."

"Good day to you."

"We would like to ask you something."

"So speak."

"How can you get along better in this world, with the truth or with lies and deceit?"

"My friends, how can one live honestly in this world? In my business, we lie a hundred times an hour and cheat our customers. That is the only way we can get ahead." And the merchant rode on.

The poor brother became sadder yet and, as they walked farther, they met a boyar.

"Good day to you, Your Kindness."

"Good day to you."

"We would like to ask something."

"Ask."

"How can we get along better in this world, by truth or by lies and deceit?"

"My dear people, where is there truth? We cannot live by it. If I were always to stay with the truth...." The boyar could not finish his sentence, and he drove off shaking his head.

"Now, brother," said the rich one, "we will go home and I will take all of your possessions."

The poor brother was very sad indeed for, when they went home, the rich brother took each and every one of his belongings, except for his little hut.

"You may live here for now," said the rich brother, "because I do not need the hut right now but, later, you will have to find another place to live."

There was no work to be had, as it had been a bad year, and the poor brother and his family had not even a crust of bread to eat. The children were crying from hunger, and he blamed himself bitterly. Eventually, he forced himself to go begging to his brother.

"Please give me some flour," he pleaded. "Some wheat, anything. We have nothing to eat, and my children are becoming ill from hunger."

The rich brother said, "Give me your right eye, and I will give you a sack of flour."

The poor brother thought and thought and, finally, he agreed. "Take it then, in the name of God."

The rich brother took the eye and gave his brother a sack of mouldy flour.

When she saw him, his wife screamed, "What happened that you lost your eye?"

"My rich brother took it for this flour," he said. And he told her the whole story. They cried together, and ate the bread she was able to bake with the flour.

A week later, the flour was all gone. The poor man took the empty sack to his brother. "Please give me more," he begged. "This is all gone and my children are starving."

"Give me your left eye, and I will fill the sack again," said the rich one.

"How can I live in this world without eyes? Can you not just give me the flour until times are better?"

"No," answered the rich man. "I cannot afford to give things away. Give me your eye."

The poor man was forced to surrender his remaining eye.

"Take it, then, in the name of God."

The rich man took the eye, filled the sack with flour and sent his brother home.

The blind man felt his away along the fence and, with much difficulty, found his way to his hut. When his wife saw him, she froze in horror. "How are you, poor soul, going to live without eyes? We could have somehow found something to eat, but your eyes...."

She cried so hard that she could no longer speak, and her husband tried to console her, saying: "Do not worry. I am not alone in this world. There are many people without eyes, and they live."

Soon, the flour sack was empty again and, once more, the children cried with hunger.

"Dear wife," said the poor man, "this time I will not go to my brother. Take me to the village and there I will sit under the elm tree. Surely someone passing by will take pity and give me a piece of bread."

The woman led him to the village; she left him under the tree, and went home.

The man sat under the tree all day with only one little scrap of bread that someone had given him. He waited and waited for his wife, but she had forgotten to come for him. He was tired unto death and wanted to go home.

The poor man began walking, and he soon became lost. When he heard the wind blowing through the branches, he realized that he was in the forest. He wanted desperately to sleep but, being afraid of wild animals, he feared to do so. Finally, he climbed into a tree as best he could, wrapped himself around a branch, and tried to sleep.

It happened that, under this same tree, some wicked imps were meeting with the chief of the imps. The chief began by asking each of them what nasty imp-deeds they had accomplished recently.

One imp spoke up: "I saw to it that one brother took both eyes from his brother in exchange for two sacks of flour."

"You have done well, but you are not finished with that yet," said the chief.

"How is it that I am not finished?"

"If the blind man were to sprinkle the dew from under this tree on his eyes, he would be able to see again."

"Well, but who knows this but us?"

The next imp said, "I have dried up all the wells in the village, and there is no water for many miles. The villagers are slowly dying."

"You have done well, but you are not finished with that yet," said the chief.

"How is it that I am not finished?"

"There is a large boulder by this tree. If the boulder were moved, enough water would flow for many villages."

"Well, but who knows this but us?"

The third imp said: "I have stricken the daughter of the tsar with an illness, and no one can help her."

"You have done well, but you are not finished with that yet," said the chief.

"How is it that I am not finished?"

"Once again, the dew from under this tree will cure her."

"Well, but who knows that but us?"

The imps and their chief then went on their way to do more mischief, unaware that the man in the tree had heard everything that had been said.

As soon as he heard their voices disappear in the distance, the man climbed down from the tree. He felt around till he found some dew, and then touched his eyes with it. He could see again!

"Now," said the man to himself, "I will go and help the others."

He gathered some dew in a large leaf, which he folded into his pocket, and then he went to the village.

Nearing the village, he saw an old woman lugging two buckets.

"Baba, I am thirsty. May I have some water, please?" he asked.

"Oh, my dear son, I have carried this water all night, and have already spilled half of it. My family will die without water."

The man said, "I am coming to the village to quench your thirst."

"How can do that?" she asked.

"Fear not; I know how to do it," he said.

The old woman left him to drink from the buckets and ran through the village telling everyone that they were saved. Some people

scoffed, but others believed. They followed her and bowed to the man, pleading, "Please, my good man, save us from a terrible death."

"I will," he said, "but I need help. Come with me, and we will see what we will see."

They went to the forest with the man and found the boulder. They put their shoulders to the boulder and strained until they moved it aside. A steady stream of water flowed from underneath the boulder. It flowed and it flowed until all the ponds, the streams and the rivers were filled once more.

The people were overjoyed, and they gave the man much money and many gifts, including a horse, which he was happy to ride.

The man immediately mounted his horse and rode to the palace of the tsar with the sick daughter. He approached the palace and told the guards: "I have heard of the illness which has struck the tsarevna, and I have come to heal her."

"Who are you that you think you can do what all the educated physicians in the country cannot do?"

"I am just a plain, honest man who can help your tsarevna. Please announce me to the tsar immediately."

The guards reluctantly did so, and the tsar eagerly received the man. "Can you heal my daughter?" he asked.

"That I can do."

"If you are successful, I will give you everything that you could ever wish for," promised the tsar.

They went to the tsarevna, who was sleeping fitfully. The man sprinkled the dew on her head. She awoke, opened her eyes, and cried, "Hello, Papa! I am hungry!"

The tsar was beside himself with joy. He had to give the man a wagon to haul home all the gifts he bestowed upon him.

Meanwhile, the poor wife had been worried all this time, and she cried constantly. She did not know what had happened to him since she had forgotten him under the elm tree in the village.

There was a sudden knock on the door, and the wife recognized the voice of her husband, who was hollering, "Open up the door, my good wife!"

Happy again, the wife ran to the door and led her husband into the hut. She looked at him and saw that his eyes were whole again. What joy she felt then!

"God in heaven!" she cried. "What a blessing! Tell me everything that has happened to you since I saw you last."

The man told her his story and showed her all the riches he had been given. Now they could live like real people!

When the rich brother heard of the good fortune his poor brother had had, he came running. "How is it that you can see? And how is it that you are now rich?" he demanded.

The man told his rich brother the whole story. Instead of feeling happy for his brother, the rich one was very jealous. He wanted to be richer than his brother.

As soon as night fell, the rich brother made his way to the tree where his brother had slept, and hid himself in the branches.

At midnight the imps and their chief appeared, and the chief said: "How can this be? Nobody knew but us! Nobody could dream up such things. And yet, the blind walk around with their eyes whole, water flows from beneath the boulder, and the tsarevna has been cured of her illness. Could it be that someone is hiding nearby and heard what we said? Let us search and find out!"

The imps and their chief searched the area, and found the man hiding in the tree. And that was the end of him!

The Wizard

There was once in our village a man named Avstriyat, who was such a wizard that he could control the weather.

One day we were cutting rye, when a cloud came up. We began to hurry with the sheaves, but Avstriyat took no notice. He cut away and smoked his pipe and said, "Do not be frightened. There will be no rain just now."

And there was no rain.

Then the sky became black and the wind began to whistle, at first far off and softly, and then right overhead and louder and louder, until we could hear nothing else but the storm. There was thunder and lightning; it was such a storm that we could only put up our hands and pray to God.

Avstriyat said, "Do not be frightened. There will be no rain." He smoked his pipe and cut away quietly.

A black man on a black horse shot across the field and darted straight up to Avstriyat. "Give permission!" he yelled.

"No, I will not," said Avstriyat, quietly.

"Give permission! Please, be merciful."

"No. We could not harvest the rye."

The black horseman bowed and raced off across the field.

The black cloud turned to gray and then to white. Our elders feared there would be hail. Avstriyat took no notice. He cut the rye and smoked his pipe. Again a horseman came tearing up to Avstriyat. He was all in white, on a white horse.

"Give permission!" he cried to Avstriyat.

"I will not."

"Give permission, please!"

"I will not. It would be impossible to get our harvest in."

"Give permission; I cannot hold out!"

Then, and not till then, did Avstriyat relent. "Well, then, go, but just in the valley."

Scarcely had he spoken when the horseman disappeared and hail poured down into the valley. In no time at all it filled the valley to the brim.

Notes on the Tales, by Danny Evanishen

Page 11   Boris Threeson

This story was translated by Angela Cleary from a German collection of Ukrainian folk tales. This is an unusual story, in that I have found it only this once, but many elements of it are very familiar. It follows to some degree the storyline of the Firebird stories found in Slavic folklore.

Page 29   The Daughter of the Flower Queen

Again, not a common story, found in only a few collections. Here we find the usual good guys and bad guys, the beautiful girl, and the magic. The ending is not the happiest one imaginable, which is quite unusual in such a tale.

Page 39   The Death of the Sun-Hero

This story is very unusual, in that our hero dies at the end. Up to that point, the story is fairly commonplace, but the moral is driven home quite forcefully with the death of the Sun-Hero.

Page 47   The Devil and the Gypsy

In Ukrainian folklore there are many stories dealing with devils. Sometimes the devil is depicted as a fierce and awful being, but more often, he is duped by our hero. Our hero this time is a gypsy, who also appears often in Ukrainian folk tales.

Page 55   The Giants and the Herdboy

This is another story that does not appear in very many collections. It has the usual magic and strange beings, but teaches us, once again, that if we are pure of heart and live honestly, good things will happen to us.

Page 63   The Hazlenut Child

This is a Thumbelina type of story, but with a Ukrainian flare. Small people have always fascinated the story audience, especially when they do as well as our Hazlenut Child. This type of story teaches us that we can succeed, no matter who we are, if we only try.

Page 69   Ivan Invisible

Another story from the German book translated by Angela Cleary. There are many tales with similar characters, and many cultures have such stories. Part of the lesson to be learned is the one the boyar and his son were taught, but one disturbing element appears that is common to many tales.

While teaching a lesson about living right and doing the right thing, the story also shows us the hero stealing from other people who have done him no harm at all. This behaviour is not explained; perhaps it is just an example of the downtrodden getting the better of others by the use of their wits or by magic.

Page 77   The Lazy Wolf

The Lazy Wolf appears in several stories, in various guises. Sometimes he is portrayed as a fool, and sometimes as just an unfortunate being. In this story, he is certainly not very bright, although he does demonstrate some ingenuity in his suggestion that the wolves climb on each other's backs to reach the tailor.

Page 87   The Lion in the Well

This is a fairly common tale. In some versions it is a rabbit and not a fox that fools the lion. Many other cultures have similar stories that teach us that might is not necessarily right.

Page 93   The Lute Player

The Lute Player is sometimes called The Harpist or some such. Whatever instrument she plays, the story is basically the same. The wife is clever enough to work her way through all sorts of difficulties and save the day. Of course, her husband at first thinks she has failed him, but he eventually sees the truth.

Page 103   The Magic Bird

From Dr Klymasz's collection, this is a fairly unusual story. Although elements of the story are very common, the story in its entirety is not. A bird with a man on its back is common, as is the hunger of the bird which must be appeased by the man in any way possible. In some stories, the cut leg magically heals when they land, and in others, like this story, little is said beyond the fact of the injury.

Page 109   The Man and the Priest

This is another of those cute little stories that are so short they appear to be more like jokes. This kind of story is obviously meant to entertain, rather than instruct; there isn't a great deal to be learned from our hero.

Page 111   The Tremendous Turnip

One of the old favorites, this tale appears in many collections and often as an illustrated book on its own. It is a delightful little story.

Page 117   Truth and Lies

From Angela Cleary's translation. Some stories of this type are fairly simple, but this one carries on until our hero is very wealthy indeed. The end is surprisingly abrupt.

Page 129   The Wizard

This story does not appear in many collections. It almost seems to be a part of a longer story, but this is pretty much the way it has been told every time I have found it.

In this glossary:

[a] is pronounced as in far
[e] is pronounced as in get
[ee] is pronounced as in feet
[i] is pronounced as in sit
[o] is pronounced as between got and goat
[oo] is pronounced as in loose
[u] is pronounced as in purr
[y] is pronounced as in yes

[kh] is pronounced as in Scottish loch
[zh] is pronounced as in vision